Writing Game Center Apps in iOS

Writing Game Center Apps in iOS

by Vandad Nahavandipoor

Copyright © 2011 Vandad Nahavandipoor. All rights reserved.
Printed in the United States of America.

Published by O'Reilly Media, Inc., 1005 Gravenstein Highway North, Sebastopol, CA 95472.

O'Reilly books may be purchased for educational, business, or sales promotional use. Online editions are also available for most titles (*http://my.safaribooksonline.com*). For more information, contact our corporate/institutional sales department: (800) 998-9938 or *corporate@oreilly.com*.

Editor: Andy Oram
Production Editor: Jasmine Perez
Proofreader: Jasmine Perez

Cover Designer: Karen Montgomery
Interior Designer: David Futato
Illustrator: Robert Romano

Printing History:

May 2011: First Edition.

ISBN: 978-1-449-30565-9

[LSI]

1303395419

Table of Contents

require permission. Answering a question by citing this book and quoting example code does not require permission. Incorporating a significant amount of example code from this book into your product's documentation does require permission.

We appreciate, but do not require, attribution. An attribution usually includes the title, author, publisher, and ISBN. For example: "*Writing Game Center Apps in iOS* by Vandad Nahavandipoor (O'Reilly). Copyright 2011 Vandad Nahavandipoor, 978-1-449-30565-9."

If you feel your use of code examples falls outside fair use or the permission given above, feel free to contact us at *permissions@oreilly.com*.

Safari® Books Online

Safari Books Online is an on-demand digital library that lets you easily search over 7,500 technology and creative reference books and videos to find the answers you need quickly.

With a subscription, you can read any page and watch any video from our library online. Read books on your cell phone and mobile devices. Access new titles before they are available for print, and get exclusive access to manuscripts in development and post feedback for the authors. Copy and paste code samples, organize your favorites, download chapters, bookmark key sections, create notes, print out pages, and benefit from tons of other time-saving features.

O'Reilly Media has uploaded this book to the Safari Books Online service. To have full digital access to this book and others on similar topics from O'Reilly and other publishers, sign up for free at *http://my.safaribooksonline.com*.

How to Contact Us

Please address comments and questions concerning this book to the publisher:

O'Reilly Media, Inc.
1005 Gravenstein Highway North
Sebastopol, CA 95472
800-998-9938 (in the United States or Canada)
707-829-0515 (international or local)
707-829-0104 (fax)

We have a web page for this book, where we list errata, examples, and any additional information. You can access this page at:

http://www.oreilly.com/catalog/0636920020349

To comment or ask technical questions about this book, send email to:

bookquestions@oreilly.com

For more information about our books, courses, conferences, and news, see our website at *http://www.oreilly.com*.

Find us on Facebook: *http://facebook.com/oreilly*

Follow us on Twitter: *http://twitter.com/oreillymedia*

Watch us on YouTube: *http://www.youtube.com/oreillymedia*

Acknowledgments

I would like to open the Acknowledgments section of this book with a sentence by Napoleon Hill:

> We are what we are, because of the vibrations of thought which we pick up and register, through the stimuli of our daily environment.

Hence, I would like to quickly say thank you to all those who have helped me become the person I am today. Thank you to Andy Oram and many thanks to Brian Jepson for their continuous support and many hours they put into working on new projects with me. I am truly grateful.

I thank Gretchen Giles, Betsy Waliszewski, and everybody at O'Reilly for recently contributing $200K to the Japanese Red Cross Society. I am truly honored to have been a part of this. This reminds me to thank Simon Whitty, Shaun Puckrin, Sushil Shirke, Gary McCarville, Kirk Pattinson, and all other colleagues of mine for being a continuous source of inspiration.

Last but not least, thank you for deciding to read this book and becoming a part of O'Reilly's new and unique way of publishing technology books. I am glad I am a part of this and that I can share my knowledge, in this case about Game Center in iOS, with you wonderful readers.

Dispatch (GCD). GCD allows developers to simply focus on the code that has to be executed and forget about the dirty work that needs to be carried out in order to balance the work among multiple threads on a device that can have multiple cores.

GCD works with block objects. Block objects are first-class functions, which means, among many other traits, that they can be passed to other methods as parameters and can be returned from methods as return values. Block objects have a syntax that differs from a simple C function or procedure. For instance, a C function that takes two int parameters (call them value1 and value2), adds them up, and returns the sum as an int can be implemented in this way:

```
int sum (int value1, int value2){
  return value1 + value2;
}
```

The equivalent of this code written using a block object would be:

```
int (^sum)(int, int) = ^(int value1, int value2){
  return value1 + value2;
};
```

Or, for instance, if we were to implement a procedure in C that simply prints out a string to the console, we would write it like this, using the printf procedure:

```
void printSomestring(void){
  printf("Some string goes here...");
}
```

The same code can be written using block objects as demonstrated here:

```
void (^printSomeString)(void) = ^(void){
  printf("Some string goes here...");
};
```

As mentioned earlier, block objects are first-class functions, and can therefore be passed to methods, procedures, and functions as parameters. For example, the sortUsingComparator: method of instances of NSMutableArray, as we will soon see, accepts block objects that return a value of type NSComparisonResult and take in two parameters each of type id. Here is how you would call that method to sort your array:

```
NSMutableArray *array = [[NSMutableArray alloc] initWithObjects:
                          @"Item 1",
                          @"Item 2",
                          @"Item 3",
                          nil];

[array sortUsingComparator:^NSComparisonResult(id obj1, id obj2) {
  /* Sort the array here and return an appropriate value */
  return NSOrderedSame;
}];

[array release];
```

In addition to passing inline block objects to other methods, it is important that you also learn how to write methods that accept and work with inline block objects passed as parameters. Let's say we have an Objective-C method, sumOf:plus:, which will take in two parameters of type NSInteger, calculate the sum, and return a 64-bit value of type long long. This Objective-C method itself will then call a block object that will calculate the sum and return the result. Here is how we can implement this:

```
long long (^sum)(NSInteger, NSInteger) =
^(NSInteger value1, NSInteger value2){

  return (long long)(value1 + value2);

};

- (long long) sumOf:(NSInteger)paramValue1
             plust:(NSInteger)paramValue2{

  return sum(paramValue1, paramValue2);

}
```

Block objects are executed just like C procedures and functions. In the case of the sum block object that we had before, we can execute it easily as shown here, inside an Objective-C method:

```
int (^sum)(int, int) = ^(int value1, int value2){
  return value1 + value2;
};

- (int) calculateSumOfTwoNumbersUsingBlockObjects:(int)number1
                            secondNumber:(int)number2{
  return sum(number1, number2);
}
```

The calculateSumOfTwoNumbersUsingBlockObjects:secondNumber: Objective-C method calls the sum block object and passes the return value of the block object to the calling code. Are you starting to see how simple block objects are? I suggest that you start writing a few block objects in your Xcode projects to just get used to the syntax. I am quite aware that the syntax of a block object is not exactly desirable as far as Objective-C developers are concerned, but once you learn the power that block objects have to offer, you will most likely forget this difficulty in constructing them and instead focus on the advantages.

One of the most important advantages to block objects is that they can be used inline and, as a result, passed to other methods as parameters. For example, if we want to sort an instance of NSMutableArray in an ascending fashion, we could use the sortUsingComparator: method of the NSMutableArray class as shown here. This method accepts a block object with two parameters and returns a value of type NSComparison Result. Because sortUsingComparator: accepts a block object as a parameter, we can use it for any kind of data and adjust the sorting method as appropriate.

We now know how to get the handle to global concurrent queues and the main queue. The big question is: how do we execute a piece of code on these queues? The answer is simple: use one of the dispatch_ procedures. Here are a few flavors for you:

dispatch_sync
Submits a block object to a given dispatch queue for synchronous execution.

dispatch_async
Submits a block object to a given dispatch queue for asynchronous execution.

dispatch_once
Submits a block object to a given dispatch queue for execution, only once during the lifetime of an application. Calling the same method and passing the same block object to any dispatch queue will return immediately without re-executing the block object.

 Block objects submitted to any of the aforementioned dispatch methods must return void and have no parameters.

Fair enough! Let's give it a go. I want to have three loops, each printing the number sequence 1 to 10, and I want to have all of them run at the same time, asynchronously. When we talk about asynchronous execution of block objects, we know we should be using the dispatch_async procedure:

```
/* Define our block object */
void (^countFrom1To10)(void) = ^{

  NSUInteger counter = 0;
  for (counter = 1;
       counter <= 10;
       counter++){
    NSLog(@"Thread = %@. Counter = %lu",
         [NSThread currentThread],
         (unsigned long)counter);
  }

};
```

The second and final piece of the puzzle is the decision as to which dispatch queue we want our code to be executed on. For this example, we can execute the code on either the main queue (run on the main thread) or better yet, on any one of the global concurrent queues. So let's go ahead and use a global concurrent queue:

```
/* Calling this method will execute the block object
 three times */
- (void) countFrom1To10ThreeTimes{

  /* Get the handle to a global concurrent queue */
  dispatch_queue_t concurrentQueue =
```

```
dispatch_get_global_queue(DISPATCH_QUEUE_PRIORITY_DEFAULT, 0);

/* Now run the block object three times */
dispatch_async(concurrentQueue, countFrom1To10);
dispatch_async(concurrentQueue, countFrom1To10);
dispatch_async(concurrentQueue, countFrom1To10);

}
```

If you invoke the countFrom1To10ThreeTimes method in your application, the results printed in the console might be similar to these:

```
...
Thread = <NSThread: 0x94312b0>{name = (null), num = 3}. Counter = 7
Thread = <NSThread: 0x9432160>{name = (null), num = 5}. Counter = 6
Thread = <NSThread: 0x9431d70>{name = (null), num = 4}. Counter = 7
Thread = <NSThread: 0x94312b0>{name = (null), num = 3}. Counter = 8
Thread = <NSThread: 0x9432160>{name = (null), num = 5}. Counter = 7
Thread = <NSThread: 0x94312b0>{name = (null), num = 3}. Counter = 9
Thread = <NSThread: 0x9431d70>{name = (null), num = 4}. Counter = 8
Thread = <NSThread: 0x9432160>{name = (null), num = 5}. Counter = 8
Thread = <NSThread: 0x94312b0>{name = (null), num = 3}. Counter = 10
Thread = <NSThread: 0x9431d70>{name = (null), num = 4}. Counter = 9
Thread = <NSThread: 0x9432160>{name = (null), num = 5}. Counter = 9
Thread = <NSThread: 0x9431d70>{name = (null), num = 4}. Counter = 10
Thread = <NSThread: 0x9432160>{name = (null), num = 5}. Counter = 10
```

The thread number for the main thread is 1; hence, looking at the thread numbers printed in this example, it can be concluded that none of the block objects were executed on the main thread. That's our proof that the global concurrent queue really did execute our block objects on threads other than the main thread. And we can conclude that the dispatch_async procedure also did its job right by executing our block objects' code asynchronously.

Now let's take a look at another example. Suppose we want to *asynchronously* download the contents of three URLs and mark the end of all the downloads by displaying an alert to our users on the user interface. The choice here between the main queue and one of the global concurrent queues is rather simple. Since the contents of the URLs could be very large, it is best not to keep the main thread busy downloading them. In other words, we should avoid using the main queue. Also, we want to download the URLs one by one. Put simply, we want to wait for the first URL to be downloaded before moving to the second one, and so on. We have the luxury of synchronous URL requests because we know that we are going to execute our block object on a global concurrent queue, which will not block the main thread. To achieve this, we shall use the dispatch_sync procedure, which will block a given queue before moving to the next block of code.

Before we can move to subjects related to Game Center, we should also take a look at the `dispatch_once` procedure discussed earlier. This procedure will execute a block object on a given dispatch queue once and only once during the lifetime of the application. There are a few things that you have to bear in mind when working with the `dispatch_once` procedure:

- This procedure is blocking. In other words, it is synchronous and will block the dispatch queue on which it runs until its code is fully executed.
- Unlike `dispatch_sync` and `dispatch_async`, this procedure does not take a dispatch queue as its parameter. By default, it will execute its task on the current dispatch queue.

 Call the `dispatch_get_current_queue` function to get the current dispatch queue.

- The first parameter to this procedure is the pointer to a value of type `dispatch_once_t`. This is how this procedure keeps track of which blocks to execute and which blocks not to execute. For instance, if you call this procedure with two different pointers for this parameter but pass the exact same block object, the block object will get executed twice because the first pointer passed each time points to different blocks of memory. If you pass the same pointer for this parameter and the same block object twice, the block object will get executed only once.
- The second parameter to this method is the block object that has to be executed. This block object has to return **void** and take no parameters.

Let's take a look at an example. Let's say I have a block object that counts from 0 to 5 and I just want it to be executed once, on a global concurrent queue to avoid blocking the main thread, during the lifetime of my application. This is how I should implement my code:

```
void (^countFrom1To5)(void) = ^(void){
  NSUInteger counter = 0;
  for (counter = 1;
       counter <= 5;
       counter++){
    NSLog(@"Thread = %@, Counter = %lu",
          [NSThread currentThread],
          (unsigned long)counter);
  }
};

- (void) countFrom1To5OnlyOnce{

  dispatch_queue_t globalQueue =
  dispatch_get_global_queue(DISPATCH_QUEUE_PRIORITY_DEFAULT, 0);
```

```
    static dispatch_once_t onceToken;

    dispatch_async(globalQueue, ^(void) {
      dispatch_once(&onceToken, countFrom1To5);
      dispatch_once(&onceToken, countFrom1To5);
    });

}
```

If I call the countFrom1To50OnlyOnce method and run my program, I will get results similar to those shown here:

```
Thread = <NSThread: 0x5f07f10>{name = (null), num = 3}, Counter = 1
Thread = <NSThread: 0x5f07f10>{name = (null), num = 3}, Counter = 2
Thread = <NSThread: 0x5f07f10>{name = (null), num = 3}, Counter = 3
Thread = <NSThread: 0x5f07f10>{name = (null), num = 3}, Counter = 4
Thread = <NSThread: 0x5f07f10>{name = (null), num = 3}, Counter = 5
```

What if I pass a different token to the dispatch_once procedure in the count From1To50OnlyOnce method?

```
Thread = <NSThread: 0x6a117f0>{name = (null), num = 3}, Counter = 1
Thread = <NSThread: 0x6a117f0>{name = (null), num = 3}, Counter = 2
Thread = <NSThread: 0x6a117f0>{name = (null), num = 3}, Counter = 3
Thread = <NSThread: 0x6a117f0>{name = (null), num = 3}, Counter = 4
Thread = <NSThread: 0x6a117f0>{name = (null), num = 3}, Counter = 5
Thread = <NSThread: 0x6a117f0>{name = (null), num = 3}, Counter = 1
Thread = <NSThread: 0x6a117f0>{name = (null), num = 3}, Counter = 2
Thread = <NSThread: 0x6a117f0>{name = (null), num = 3}, Counter = 3
Thread = <NSThread: 0x6a117f0>{name = (null), num = 3}, Counter = 4
Thread = <NSThread: 0x6a117f0>{name = (null), num = 3}, Counter = 5
```

The code in this example was executed twice. Not what we wanted. So make sure that, for whatever block of code that has to be executed once, you pass the same pointer to the first parameter of the dispatch_once procedure.

You should now have a good understanding of block objects and GCD, so we can dive right into more interesting subjects concerning Game Center. Here are a few links if you require further information about block objects and GCD:

- Introducing Blocks and Grand Central Dispatch (*https://developer.apple.com/li brary/mac/#featuredarticles/BlocksGCD/_index.html*)
- Grand Central Dispatch (GCD) Reference (*https://developer.apple.com/library/ mac/#documentation/Performance/Reference/GCD_libdispatch_Ref/Reference/ref erence.html*)

See Also

Recipe 1.2; Recipe 1.3

other players to find you on Game Center using your email address, switch on Find Me By Email. You can also add other email addresses to the list that your account is associated with so players can find your Game Center account using any of these addresses. Once you are finished, press the Done button on the navigation bar.

9. The Game Center app on the iOS Simulator will now log you into Game Center and display the main Game Center interface, as shown in Figure 1-2.

Figure 1-2. The main Game Center interface, once logged in

 The leftmost tab in the Game Center app (once you have logged in) says "Sandbox," denoting that you are indeed using the sandbox environment.

Now go ahead and create at least one more Game Center player on the sandbox environment. To test the example code in this book, you will ideally need three sandbox players. If you are reluctant to spend time registering three players, you must at least create two. Otherwise, you will not be able to test about 90 percent of the example code.

See Also

Recipe 1.5

1.3 Setting Up Game Center for an iOS App

Problem

You want to be able to connect to the Game Center servers in your iOS apps.

Solution

You need to create your app in iTunes Connect and also set your app's bundle identifier both in iTunes Connect and your app's *info.plist* file as demonstrated in the Discussion section.

Discussion

In Recipe 1.2, we created sandbox Game Center accounts using the Game Center iOS App, which is installed on all instances of iOS Simulator. That was the first piece of the puzzle. The next is setting up our iOS App with Game Center using iTunes Connect. This might confuse you a bit at first. The linchpin is to create an app in Xcode and give it a bundle identifier. For instance, here is the bundle identifier that I am using:

```
com.pixolity.testgame
```

Setting the identifier in your app bundle won't do the trick by itself. You have to set up your application on iTunes Connect. Set the app's bundle identifier on iTunes Connect to the same identifier you set in your application bundle in Xcode.

We'll handle these tasks in this section, but we will *not* upload the app to iTunes Connect. By following the procedure in this section, you'll set up your app on iTunes in the state of *Prepare for Upload*. You will be able to access Game Center for the app. But because it is not actually uploaded to iTunes Connect, your Game Center connections will run on the sandbox environment. The same code will run on the production server in a later stage, after your app has been uploaded to iTunes Connect.

Follow these steps to set up an iOS app with Game Center on iTunes Connect:

1. Sign in to Apple Developer Portal (*http://developer.apple.com/devcenter/ios/index.action*) using your developer credentials.
2. Once you are logged in, select iOS Provision Portal from the righthand side.
3. In the portal, select App IDs from the lefthand side menu.
4. Press the New App ID button.
5. In the New App ID screen, give your new App ID a description. This can be anything you want that describes your application.

    In the Bundle Seed ID (App ID Prefix) section, select the Generate New item. This will generate a new bundle seed ID for your application. The application bundle (which we talked about earlier) appended to this seed ID will form a unique name that identifies your application. For instance, if you leave this option up to Generate

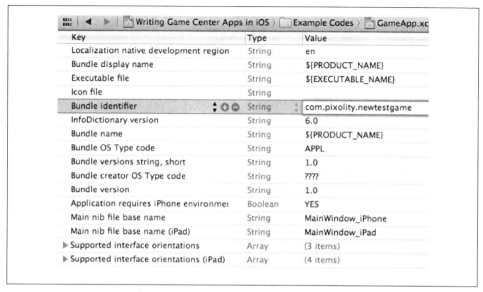

Key	Type	Value
Localization native development region	String	en
Bundle display name	String	${PRODUCT_NAME}
Executable file	String	${EXECUTABLE_NAME}
Icon file	String	
Bundle identifier	String	com.pixolity.newtestgame
InfoDictionary version	String	6.0
Bundle name	String	${PRODUCT_NAME}
Bundle OS Type code	String	APPL
Bundle versions string, short	String	1.0
Bundle creator OS Type code	String	????
Bundle version	String	1.0
Application requires iPhone environmei	Boolean	YES
Main nib file base name	String	MainWindow_iPhone
Main nib file base name (iPad)	String	MainWindow_iPad
▶ Supported interface orientations	Array	(3 items)
▶ Supported interface orientations (iPad)	Array	(4 items)

Figure 1-5. Setting the Bundle Identifier of an app in Xcode 4

1.4 Adding the Game Kit Framework

Problem

You have set up your project and want to start incorporating Game Center APIs into your app.

Solution

Add the Game Kit framework to your app as demonstrated in the Discussion section.

Discussion

To use Game Center's capabilities, you must link your application against the Game Kit framework. Assuming you have created an Xcode project already for this app, import this framework into your Xcode project as follows:

1. Click on your project (which should have a blueish icon) in Xcode. Once you see your project's settings, click on the target that has to be linked against the Game Kit framework.

2. On the top of the screen, select Build Phases and then expand the Link Binary With Libraries box, as shown in Figure 1-6.

3. Click on the + button, select GameKit.framework from the list, and press the Add button, as depicted in Figure 1-7.

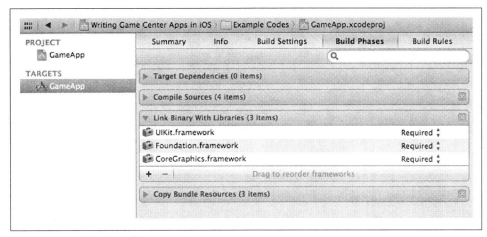

Figure 1-6. Build Phases for an iOS app

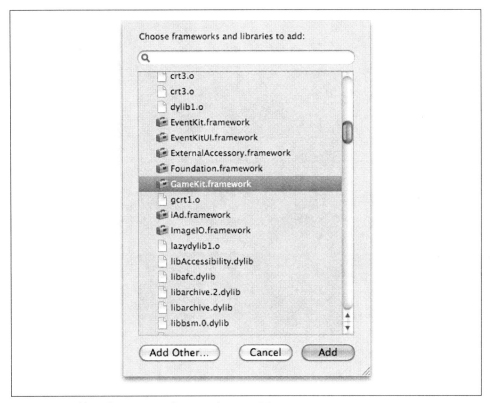

Figure 1-7. Adding the Game Kit framework to an iOS target

If the player has not authenticated herself yet, attempting to retrieve the local player will prompt the player to authenticate first. If the player cancels, we will get an error back in our code. If the player has already authenticated, she won't be prompted to log into Game Center again. So long as she is authenticated, we will be able to retrieve her player object.

Every player in Game Center is represented with an object of GKPlayer. The local player is also a player, but is represented with an object of type GKLocalPlayer, a subclass of the GKPlayer class. In order to retrieve a reference to the local player object, you can use the localPlayer class method of the GKLocalPlayer class like so:

```
GKLocalPlayer *localPlayer = [GKLocalPlayer localPlayer];
```

After you have the local player's object, you must, as soon as you have the ability to do so (right after your application loads), authenticate the player using the authenticate WithCompletionHandler: instance method of the GKLocalPlayer class. This method accepts a block object that should have no return value and should accept a single parameter of type NSError that will store any error that occurs during the authentication process:

```
- (void) authenticateLocalPlayer{

    GKLocalPlayer *localPlayer = [GKLocalPlayer localPlayer];

    [localPlayer authenticateWithCompletionHandler:^(NSError *error) {

      if (error == nil){
        NSLog(@"Successfully authenticated the local player.");
      } else {
        NSLog(@"Failed to authenticate the player with error = %@", error);
      }

    }];

}
```

If the player has not logged into Game Center, after the execution of this code, she will be prompted with a dialog asking her to do so. This is depicted in Figure 1-8.

The isAuthenticated instance method of the GKLocalPlayer class returns YES if the local player has already authenticated and NO if she has not. So, in order to improve our authentication method, we can add this factor in:

```
- (void) authenticateLocalPlayer{

    GKLocalPlayer *localPlayer = [GKLocalPlayer localPlayer];

    if ([localPlayer isAuthenticated] == YES){
      NSLog(@"The local player has already authenticated.");
      return;
    }

    [localPlayer authenticateWithCompletionHandler:^(NSError *error) {
```

Figure 1-8. Game Center, asking the local player to log in

```
    if (error == nil){
      NSLog(@"Successfully authenticated the local player.");
    } else {
      NSLog(@"Failed to authenticate the player with error = %@", error);
    }

  }];

}
```

We are calling the isAuthenticated instance method of the GKLocal
Player class to avoid attempting to authenticate the player over and
over again. Leaving out this check will not bother the player because, if
she has already logged into Game Center, the dialog displayed in
Figure 1-8 will not get displayed again. But doing the check saves us a
wasted call to Game Center.

Now that you know how to authenticate the local player, it is time to move to more
sophisticated subjects in Game Center, such as Recipe 1.6.

See Also

Recipe 1.6

1.7 Adding Friends in Game Center

Problem

You have learned to authenticate the local player, but to test Game Center APIs on other players, you want to add some friends to the local player's account.

Solution

Use the iOS Simulator built-in Game Center app to add friends to the local player, as demonstrated in the Discussion section.

Discussion

To add a friend in Game Center on the sandbox server, follow these steps:

1. Open the iOS Simulator if it's not already open.
2. Open the Game Center app in the Simulator.
3. Log in, if you are not logged in already.
4. Once logged in, from the bottom of the screen, select the Friends tab.
5. Press + on the navigation bar.
6. In the Friend Request screen, type the nickname or the email address of the friends you want to add to your list.
7. Once done, press Send on the navigation bar in the top righthand corner.
8. Game Center will then let you know whether it could send the invites or not.

It just couldn't be simpler than this!

See Also

Recipe 1.8

1.8 Retrieving the Local Player's Friends Information

Problem

You've added friends to the local player's Game Center account, but now you want to enumerate them and retrieve their information, such as their alias.

Solution

Use the `friends` property of the local player's object, an instance of `GKLocalPlayer`.

Discussion

The GKLocalPlayer class has a property called friends of type NSArray. This property will contain the players that the local player is friends with. The array represents the players using their player IDs (explained in Recipe 1.6).

I said *will* in the previous paragraph because, after authentication of the local player, this array is empty (nil). You need to call the loadFriendsWithCompletionHandler: instance method of the GKLocalPlayer class to load the player ID for each of the local player's friends. After retrieving the IDs, call another method to retrieve other information for each friend based on his or her player ID.

The loadFriendsWithCompletionHandler: instance method of the GKLocalPlayer class accepts one parameter, which should be a block that returns void (or in other words, doesn't return anything). This block object will have two parameters. The first is of type NSArray and will, upon return, contain the friend IDs of the local player. The second is of type NSError and will indicate whether an error occurred during the process.

 To avoid repeating code over and over, I assume that you have already authenticated the local player using the material taught in Recipe 1.5.

Let's take a look at an example where we just load the local player's friends' IDs:

```
void (^getLocalPlayerFriends)(void) = ^{

  GKLocalPlayer *localPlayer = [GKLocalPlayer localPlayer];

  if ([localPlayer isAuthenticated] == NO){
    NSLog(@"The local player is not authenticated.");
    return;
  }

  NSLog(@"Loading local player's friend IDs...");
  [localPlayer loadFriendsWithCompletionHandler:
   ^(NSArray *friends, NSError *error) {

     if (friends != nil){
       NSLog(@"Successfully retrieved friends of the local player.");
       NSUInteger counter = 1;
       for (NSString *friendID in friends){
         NSLog(@"Friend %lu = %@", (unsigned long)counter, friendID);
         counter++;
       }
     }

     if (error != nil){
       NSLog(@"Error occurred. Error = %@", error);
     }
```

```
    };

    - (void) authenticateLocalPlayerAndGetHerInfo{

      dispatch_queue_t concurrentQueue =
        dispatch_get_global_queue(DISPATCH_QUEUE_PRIORITY_DEFAULT, 0);

      dispatch_async(concurrentQueue, ^(void) {
        GKLocalPlayer *localPlayer = [GKLocalPlayer localPlayer];
        if ([localPlayer isAuthenticated] == NO){
          [localPlayer authenticateWithCompletionHandler:^(NSError *error) {
            if (error == nil){
              NSLog(@"Successfully authenticated.");
              dispatch_async(concurrentQueue, getLocalPlayerFriends);
            } else {
              NSLog(@"Failed to authenticate. Error = %@", error);
            }
          }];
        } else {
          dispatch_async(concurrentQueue, getLocalPlayerFriends);
        }
      });

    }
```

After calling the authenticateLocalPlayerAndGetHerInfo method in this example code,
I get the following results (because I authenticate the local player, who has two friends
in her list):

```
Successfully authenticated.
Loading local player's friend IDs...
Successfully retrieved friends of the local player.
Loading players...
Successfully loaded the players.
<GKPlayer 0x5f32d90>(playerID: G:1428629254, alias: Test Game User 2,
    status: (null), rid:(null))
<GKPlayer 0x5f32cf0>(playerID: G:1428629742, alias: Test Game User 3,
    status: (null), rid:(null))
```

Once you have this information, you can either display it to the player or keep it for
future reference. With regard to player IDs, please do not store these in your game.
Whenever the player runs your app, you must attempt to retrieve the fresh list of friends
instead of assuming the friends that your app retrieved a few days ago are still the local
player's friends. Also, the format of the player ID might change, as Apple has mentioned
in its documentation:

> Do not make assumptions about the contents of the player identifier string. Its format
> and length are subject to change.

> —Game Center Documentation

See Also

Recipe 1.5

1.9 Creating Leaderboards in iTunes Connect

Problem

You don't know how to start incorporating leaderboards into your iOS games.

Solution

Set up leaderboards in iTunes Connect.

Discussion

One of the functionalities in Game Center is the ability to manage leaderboards in your iOS apps. For instance, you can write a racing game for iOS and have players compete to achieve the best score. You can then report these scores to a leaderboard and allow the players to see the leaderboard. This gives your players a reason to come back to your app (in order to compete with their friends).

To use leaderboards in your app, you must first create them for your app in iTunes Connect. Here is how you can do that:

1. Go to the Apple Developer Portal (*http://developer.apple.com/devcenter/ios/index .action*) and select iTunes Connect from the righthand side of the screen.

2. In iTunes Connect, select Manage Your Applications.

3. In Manage Your Applications, select the app you want to add a leaderboard to. To add a leaderboard to an app, you must have already enabled Game Center for it (Figure 1-4).

4. Once in the app in iTunes Connect, select the Manage Game Center button on the righthand side of the screen.

5. Under Leaderboard box, select the Set Up button.

6. Select the Add Leaderboard button on the top lefthand corner.

There are two types of leaderboards in Game Center:

Single Leaderboard
> A leaderboad that you report scores to and retrieve scores from. This can be, for instance, a leaderboard for one of the levels in your game. Level 1 of your game can have one leaderboard, Level 2 can have another, and so on.

Combined Leaderboard
> This is a leaderboard that merges data from two or more leaderboards. For instance, if you have ten levels in your game and one leaderboard per level (that is,

Solution

Use the `reportScoreWithCompletionHandler:` instance method of the `GKScore` class as demonstrated in the Discussion section.

Discussion

Assuming that you have already created a leaderboard (see Recipe 1.9), you must follow these steps to report scores to it:

1. Authenticate the local player (see Recipe 1.5).
2. Create an instance of the `GKScore` class and set the category of that score to the Leaderboard ID that you chose when you were creating this leaderboard.
3. Set the `value` property of the score object.
4. Use the `reportScoreWithCompletionHandler:` instance method of the `GKScore` class to report the error. This method accepts one parameter, which must be a block that returns **void** and accepts a parameter of type **NSError**. You can use this error to determine whether an error occurred during the process of reporting the score:

```
- (BOOL) reportScore:(NSUInteger)paramScore
      toLeaderboard:(NSString *)paramLeaderboard{

  __block BOOL result = NO;

  GKLocalPlayer *localPlayer = [GKLocalPlayer localPlayer];

  if ([localPlayer isAuthenticated] == NO){
    NSLog(@"You must authenticate the local player first.");
    return NO;
  }

  if ([paramLeaderboard length] == 0){
    NSLog(@"Leaderboard identifier is empty.");
    return NO;
  }

  GKScore *score = [[[GKScore alloc]
                    initWithCategory:paramLeaderboard] autorelease];

  score.value = (int64_t)paramScore;

  NSLog(@"Attempting to report the score...");

  [score reportScoreWithCompletionHandler:^(NSError *error) {
    if (error == nil){
      NSLog(@"Succeeded in reporting the error.");
      result = YES;
    } else {
      NSLog(@"Failed to report the error. Error = %@", error);
    }
  }];
```

```
      return result;

    }

    - (void) authenticateLocalPlayerAndReportScore{

      GKLocalPlayer *localPlayer = [GKLocalPlayer localPlayer];

      if ([localPlayer isAuthenticated] == YES){
        NSLog(@"The local player has already authenticated.");
        return;
      }

      [localPlayer authenticateWithCompletionHandler:^(NSError *error) {

        if (error == nil){
          NSLog(@"Successfully authenticated the local player.");

          [self reportScore:10
              toLeaderboard:@"MGL1LB"];

        } else {
          NSLog(@"Failed to authenticate the player with error = %@", error);
        }

      }];

    }
```

Calling the authenticateLocalPlayerAndReportScore method will attempt to authenticate the local player and then report the score of 10 to a leaderboard with Reference ID of MGL1LB (see Recipe 1.9). Here are the results that I see printed to my console window:

```
Successfully authenticated the local player.
Attempting to report the score...
Succeeded in reporting the error.
```

If you try reporting a score to a nonexistent leaderboard, the error that you will receive from the reportScoreWithCompletionHandler: method will be similar to this:

```
Error Domain=GKErrorDomain Code=17 "The requested operations could
not be completed because one or more parameters are invalid."
UserInfo=0x5f43a90 {NSUnderlyingError=0x5f09390 "The operation
couldn't be completed. status = 5053", NSLocalizedDescription=The
requested operations could not be completed because
one or more parameters are invalid.}
```

There are three ways you can see the scores that you have reported to Game Center (sandbox server):

- Using the Game Center app on iOS Simulator.
- Retrieving the scores programmatically (see Recipe 1.11).
- Displaying leaderboards in your app's user interface (see Recipe 1.12).

parameter to this block is an instance of NSArray, which will contain the scores that were loaded from the given leaderboard. The second parameter is of type NSError, which will contain an error (if any).

 Game Center might, under certain circumstances, return a valid array of scores to you and, at the same time, an error. This means that, although some of the scores were retrieved successfully, an error occurred while the scores were being fetched from Game Center. In this case, Game Center stops as soon as it receives the error and you will get *some* of the scores, not all of them.

Each leaderboard score in Game Center is encapsulated into an instance of GKScore, as we saw in Recipe 1.10. Let's take a look at example code retrieving scores from a leaderboard with Reference ID (category) of MGL1LB:

```
GKLocalPlayer *localPlayer = [GKLocalPlayer localPlayer];

  NSLog(@"Authenticating the local player...");
  [localPlayer authenticateWithCompletionHandler:^(NSError *error) {

    if (error == nil){

      NSLog(@"Successfully authenticated the local player.");
      GKLeaderboard *leaderboard =
        [[[GKLeaderboard alloc] init] autorelease];

      [leaderboard setCategory:@"MGL1LB"];
      NSLog(@"Loading the scores in leaderboard...");
      [leaderboard loadScoresWithCompletionHandler:
       ^(NSArray *scores, NSError *error) {

         if (scores != nil){
           for (GKScore *score in scores){
             NSLog(@"%@", score);
           }
         }

         if (error != nil){
           NSLog(@"Error occurred = %@", error);
         }

      }];

    } else {
      NSLog(@"Failed to authenticate with error = %@", error);
    }

  }];
```

After reporting the score 10, 20, and 35 for three Game Center players (who are all friends of each other) in Recipe 1.10 and executing this code, the console window will print following similar to this:

```
Authenticating the local player...
Successfully authenticated the local player.
Loading the scores in leaderboard...
GKScore player=G:1428629742 rank=1 date=2011-03-27
       10:39:58 +0000 value=35 formattedValue=35points
GKScore player=G:1428629254 rank=2 date=2011-03-27
       10:39:24 +0000 value=20 formattedValue=20points
GKScore player=G:1428628142 rank=3 date=2011-03-27
       09:21:19 +0000 value=10 formattedValue=10points
```

See Also

Recipe 1.12

1.12 Displaying Leaderboards to Players

Problem

You want to display leaderboards to your app users using a graphical user interface.

Solution

Use the GKLeaderboardViewController class as shown in the Discussion section.

Discussion

Game Center can construct built-in leaderboard screens for your games. Doing this is a piece of cake for Game Center. All you have to do is build an iOS application that makes use of view controllers. This is outside the scope of this book, but is thoroughly explained in iOS 4 Programming Cookbook (*http://oreilly.com/catalog/ 0636920010180/*). For the remainder of this section, I assume you have created an application with one view controller inside a navigation controller.

To have Game Center construct a leaderboard screen for your iOS app, follow these steps:

1. Make sure that you have a view controller in your application (see iOS 4 Programming Cookbook (*http://oreilly.com/catalog/0636920010180/*)). Also make sure that your view controller conforms to the GKLeaderboardViewControllerDelegate protocol.

2. Authenticate the local player (see Recipe 1.5).

3. Allocate and instantiate an object of type GKLeaderboardViewController and present it to the player using the presentModalViewController:animated: instance method of your view controller.

4. Implement the leaderboardViewControllerDidFinish: delegate method of the GKLeaderboardViewControllerDelegate protocol in your view controller.

1.13 Creating Achievements in iTunes Connect

Problem

You want your game's users to keep coming back to your app by allowing them to unlock achievements inside your game.

Solution

Use iTunes Connect to create achievements for your game, as demonstrated in the Discussion section.

Discussion

Game Center allows iOS developers to include achievements in their apps and record the player's progress toward completing an achievement. For instance, you might be writing a first person shooter game. In your game, you have a normal map that the player can walk through and engage in battles with the opponent. You might have decided to include some *hidden* paths in your game that not everybody can find. Only those who have been playing the game long enough know about these hidden paths. When a player finds a hidden path for the first time, you can report an achievement to the Game Center and give the player some reward in order to keep her interested in the game. The player can then work toward completing that achievement, as each achievement can have a completion percentage.

Let's consider a simple scenario. Let's say I find the hidden path in the game. Suppose the game requires me not only to find the path, but also to go to the end of the path for the achievement to be unlocked. When the player finds the path, you can report 0 percent for that achievement. Once the player is halfway through the path, you can report 50 percent for that achievement, and once she goes through the road and comes out of the other side, you can mark that achievement 100 percent completed.

You can have two different types of achievements:

Normal
These will appear in the player's list of achievements as soon as a progress has been reported by your app to the Game Center, even if it is 0 percent.

Hidden
These cannot be seen by the player unless the progress reported to Game Center by your app is 100 percent.

To add achievements to your app, you must first create them for your app in iTunes Connect. Here is how you can do that:

1. Go to the Apple Developer Portal (*http://developer.apple.com/devcenter/ios/index .action*) and select iTunes Connect from the righthand side of the screen.

2. In iTunes Connect, select Manage Your Applications.

---

3. In Manage Your Applications, select the app you want to add an achievement to. To add an achievement to an app, you must have already enabled Game Center for it (Figure 1-4).

4. Once in the app in iTunes Connect, select the Manage Game Center button on the righthand side of the screen.

5. In the Achievements box, select the Set Up button.

6. Select the Add New Achievement button on the top lefthand corner.

7. In the Achievement Reference Name box, enter a name that you would like to use to refer to this achievement. This will *not* be the name you will be using to refer to this achievement in your code. This is simply a name you can see later in iTunes Connect. Pick a descriptive name such as "My Game's Level 1 Hidden Path 1 Completed."

8. In the Achievement ID box, enter the ID that you will use later in your code to refer to this achievement. For instance, I could pick MGL1HP1C (referring to "My Game's Level 1 Hidden Path 1 Completed," which I picked as the reference name). Pick any reference ID you want, and use it later in your app to refer to this achievement.

9. If you want this achievement to be a hidden achievement, select Yes; otherwise, select No. For this example, please select No.

10. In the Point Value box, select 100.

 All achievements for an app combined together can have a maximum number of 1,000 points. Each achievement by itself can have a maximum of 100 points.

The Game Center app displays achievements (with at least one progress reported) to the player. A player will be able to see a normal achievement in her list even before completing it. Let's say you are working on a racing game with AI-controlled cars, and one of the achievements goes to players who can win against them 10 times in a row. As soon as the player wins against the computer once, you can report a completion progress of 10 percent (one-tenth of the final achievement). At this point, the player can log into the Game Center app and see this achievement in his list. Game Center will *not* say that this achievement has been completed, because the completion progress is not 100 percent. What it will say, however, is how the player can work to complete this achievement, a description you should provide. Once the player wins against the AI-driven car 10 times in a row, Game Center will show that he has received this achievement successfully. Because you should provide descriptions of the achievement when the first progress is displayed and after the player completes the achievement, you need to use the *localization* feature in iTunes Connect as follows:

11. Select the Add Language button.

12. Pick English in the Language box (Figure 1-13).

```
    NSLog(@"Reporting the achievement...");
    [achievement reportAchievementWithCompletionHandler:^(NSError *error) {

        if (error == nil){
          NSLog(@"Successfully reported the achievement.");
        } else {
          NSLog(@"Failed to report the achievement. %@", error);
        }

    }];

    return result;

}

- (void) authenticateLocalPlayerAndReportAchievement{

    GKLocalPlayer *localPlayer = [GKLocalPlayer localPlayer];

    NSLog(@"Authenticating the local player...");
    [localPlayer authenticateWithCompletionHandler:^(NSError *error) {

        if (error == nil){
          NSLog(@"Successfully authenticated the local player.");
          NSLog(@"Reporting achievement...");
          [self reportAchievementWithID:@"MGL1HP1C"
                    percentageCompleted:50.0f];
        } else {
          NSLog(@"Failed to authenticate the local player. %@", error);
        }

    }];

}
```

After calling the authenticateLocalPlayerAndReportAchievement method, you will get results printed to the console window similar to these shown here (unless there is an error, in which case the errors will get printed to the console window):

```
Authenticating the local player...
Successfully authenticated the local player.
Reporting achievement...
Setting percentage to 50.00
Reporting the achievement...
Successfully reported the achievement.
```

After an achievement is reported to Game Center, if the achievement wasn't set up as a hidden achievement, the local player can open the Game Center app and take a look at it, along with all the achievements she has collected while using your app, as shown in Figure 1-14.

Once the player selects the Achievements option, she will see all the achievements that an app has reported to Game Center and the progress along each achievement, as shown in Figure 1-15.

Figure 1-14. Achievements on iOS Simulator

Figure 1-15. Achievement progress on iOS Simulator

have, as parameters, an instance of NSArray that will contain the achievements and an instance of NSError that will contain any errors that occur. Here is example code:

```objc
- (void) authenticateAndGetAchievementsInfo{

    GKLocalPlayer *localPlayer = [GKLocalPlayer localPlayer];

    NSLog(@"Authenticating the local player...");
    [localPlayer authenticateWithCompletionHandler:^(NSError *error) {

        if (error == nil){
            NSLog(@"Successfully authenticated the local player.");

            [GKAchievementDescription
             loadAchievementDescriptionsWithCompletionHandler:
             ^(NSArray *descriptions, NSError *error) {

                NSUInteger counter = 1;
                for (GKAchievementDescription *description in descriptions){
                    NSLog(@"Achievement %lu. Description = %@",
                          (unsigned long)counter,
                          descriptions);
                    counter++;
                }

            }];

        } else {
            NSLog(@"Failed to authenticate the local player. %@", error);
        }

    }];

}
```

Here is an example of what the authenticateAndGetAchievementsInfo method could print out to the console window:

```
Authenticating the local player...
Successfully authenticated the local player.
Achievement 1. Description = (
    "id: MGL1HP1C\tvisible\tYou came out of
        Hidden Path 1 alive. Great job.",

    "id: MGL1HP2C\tvisible\tYou found Hidden
        Path 2. Congratulations."
)
Achievement 2. Description = (
    "id: MGL1HP1C\tvisible\tYou came out of
        Hidden Path 1 alive. Great job.",

    "id: MGL1HP2C\tvisible\tYou found Hidden
        Path 2. Congratulations."
)
```

The achievement description objects contain an ID which you can match against the achievement objects we retrieved earlier. Here is how you can retrieve achievements and match them against their descriptions:

1. Retrieve the list of achievements in objects of type GKAchievement, as we saw earlier.
2. Use the loadAchievementDescriptionsWithCompletionHandler: class method of the GKAchievementDescription class to retrieve the description of all achievements.
3. Finally, match the descriptions with the achievement objects that you retrieved earlier.

See Also

Recipe 1.14; Recipe 1.16

1.16 Displaying Achievements to Players

Problem

You need to display the achievements that the local player has received or is in the progress of receiving, using a graphical user interface.

Solution

Use the GKAchievementViewController class.

Discussion

Game Center can construct built-in achievements screens for your games. All you have to do is to build an iOS application that makes use of view controllers, covered in iOS 4 Programming Cookbook (*http://oreilly.com/catalog/0636920010180/*). For the remainder of this section, I assume you have created an application with one view controller inside a navigation controller.

In order to have Game Center construct an achievement screen for your iOS app, follow these steps:

1. Make sure that you have a view controller in your application (see iOS 4 Programming Cookbook (*http://oreilly.com/catalog/0636920010180/*)). Also make sure your view controller conforms to the GKAchievementViewControllerDelegate protocol.
2. Authenticate the local player (see Recipe 1.5).

1.17 Supporting Multiplayer Games and Matchmaking

Problem

You want to allow multiple players to join the same game and play your game together.

Solution

Incorporate matchmaking in your app, as explained in the Discussion section.

Discussion

One of the most important functionalities provided to iOS developers in Game Center is matchmaking. Matchmaking allows two or more players to play the same game in multiplayer mode at the same time. You can either use Apple's servers for multiplayer games or host your own server. In this book, we will only cover matchmaking using Apple's server, for the sake of simplicity.

 Sending matchmaking invites is not possible from the iOS Simulator. Since matchmaking is between two or more players, you need at least two real iOS devices to test it, even on Sandbox servers. For the examples in this section, I am testing the code on an iPhone 4 and an iPad 2.

There are two essential programming activities in a multiplayer game using Game Center:

1. Creating, waiting for, and accepting new match requests.
2. Transmitting game data during play.

The first part is perhaps the more difficult one to understand. To make it easier for you, let me paint a rather general picture of how things work in multiplayer mode in Game Center. When your app runs on an iOS device, it must:

1. Authenticate the local player (see Recipe 1.5).
2. Tell Game Center which block of code has to be executed, if an invitation is received from Game Center. This block of code (a block object) will be stored in Game Center locally on the device. When your application is not even running and a new invitation comes to the local player, Game Center will start your app and execute the given block of code that you have provided. Learn this and you've learned *50 percent of all there is to know about matchmaking in Game Center*.
3. Handle delegate messages for each match: messages such as state changes for players playing the game. For instance, if you are in the middle of a match and a player gets disconnected, you will receive a specific match delegate.

4. Once the match has started, you will be able to use the match object to send data to other players, or to all of them at the same time. The match delegate methods will get called on other players' devices when new data comes through. The app can then read that data (encapsulated in an instance of NSData) and act upon it.

Before we jump into coding, please make sure the following conditions have been met:

- Have at least two iOS devices ready for development.
- Assign a bundle ID to your application, as described in Recipe 1.3.
- You must have created a provision profile for your application. Follow these steps to do so:
    1. Go to the Apple Developer Portal (*http://developer.apple.com/devcenter/ios/in dex.action*) and in the righthand side of the screen, select iOS Provision Portal.
    2. Select Provisioning from the lefthand side.
    3. In the Development tab, select the New Profile button on the righthand side to land in the Create iOS Development Provisioning Profile screen (Figure 1-17).

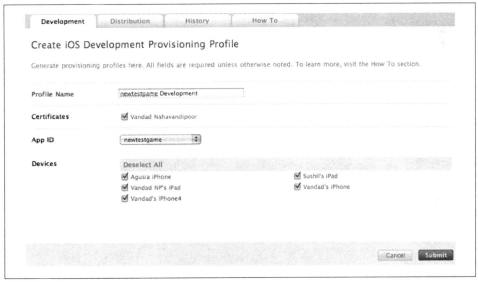

Figure 1-17. Creating a new development provision profile

4. In the Profile Name, choose a name for your profile. This name will be visible in Xcode so you know which profile you are choosing.
5. For Certificates, select your developer certificate. Usually you will see only one item here, so check that item.
6. In the App ID dropdown, select the App ID that you created for your app in Recipe 1.3.

```
- (void)dealloc{
  [acceptedMatch release];
  [buttonSendData release];
  [textViewIncomingData release];
  [textViewIncomingData release];
  [super dealloc];
}
```

6. In the `viewDidLoad` instance method of your view controller, authenticate the local player (see Recipe 1.5):

```
- (void) viewDidLoad{
  [super viewDidLoad];

  GKLocalPlayer *localPlayer = [GKLocalPlayer localPlayer];

  [localPlayer authenticateWithCompletionHandler:^(NSError *error) {

    if (error == nil){

      /* We will write the rest of this code soon */

    } else {
      NSLog(@"Failed to authenticate the player. Error = %@", error);
    }

  }];

}
```

7. As soon as the player is successfully authenticated, you should, as was mentioned earlier, tell Game Center how you want to respond to incoming matchmaking requests. Declare an instance method called `setInviteHandler` and in it, set the `inviteHandler` of the shared matchmaker object, as shown here:

```
- (void) setInviteHandler{

  [GKMatchmaker sharedMatchmaker].inviteHandler =
  ^(GKInvite *acceptedInvite, NSArray *playersToInvite) {

  };

}
```

8. The `acceptedInvite` parameter passed to this block object will get set if an invitation has been sent by another player playing the same game to start a multiplayer match. In this case, you have to present the matchmaking view controller, as we shall soon see. The `playersToInvite` parameter will get set to an array of players that have requested matchmaking on your application through the Game Center app, in which case the Game Center app will wake your application up and ask it to handle

the request. When this happens, you should also present the matchmaking view controller, but we will initialize the view controller differently:

```objc
- (void) setInviteHandler{

  [GKMatchmaker sharedMatchmaker].inviteHandler =
  ^(GKInvite *acceptedInvite, NSArray *playersToInvite) {

    if (acceptedInvite != nil){

      NSLog(@"An invite came through. process it...");

      GKMatchmakerViewController *controller =
        [[[GKMatchmakerViewController alloc]
          initWithInvite:acceptedInvite] autorelease];

      [controller setMatchmakerDelegate:self];
      [self presentModalViewController:controller
                              animated:YES];

    }

    else if (playersToInvite != nil){

      NSLog(@"Game Center invoked our game. process the match...");

      GKMatchRequest *matchRequest =
        [[[GKMatchRequest alloc] init] autorelease];

      [matchRequest setPlayersToInvite:playersToInvite];
      [matchRequest setMinPlayers:2];
      [matchRequest setMaxPlayers:2];


      GKMatchmakerViewController *controller =
        [[[GKMatchmakerViewController alloc]
          initWithMatchRequest:matchRequest] autorelease];

      [controller setMatchmakerDelegate:self];
      [self presentModalViewController:controller
                              animated:YES];
    }
  };

}
```

9. Every time our view controller's view is loaded, we decide to authenticate the local player. In addition to that, after the local player's authentication, we have to now set the invitation handler for new Game Center invites by calling the setInviteHandler instance method. In addition to that, we want to display a matchmaking view controller to the player as soon as she opens the app. So imagine two players opening the app at the same time. The first thing they will see is the matchmaking view controller asking them to start a match with another person:

```
   didFailWithError:(NSError *)error{

}
```

 For more information about players' states during a multiplayer match, please refer to Recipe 1.18.

12. The `match:didReceiveData:fromPlayer:` delegate method of the match object gets called whenever the local player receives incoming data from a player in the current match. In this method, we want to receive the incoming data, turn it into a string, and append it to the end of the text we are currently displaying on our text view. For instance, if a player sends the data "I am Ready to Start Level 1" the first time and then "I Finished Level 1" the next time, we will display "I am Ready to Start Level 1" as the first line and "I Finished Level 1" as the second line inside our text view:

```
/* The match received data sent from the player. */
- (void)  match:(GKMatch *)match
 didReceiveData:(NSData *)data
     fromPlayer:(NSString *)playerID{

  NSLog(@"Incoming data from player ID = %@", playerID);

  NSString *incomingDataAsString =
    [[NSString alloc] initWithData:data
                          encoding:NSUTF8StringEncoding];

  NSString *existingText = self.textViewIncomingData.text;

  NSString *finalText =
    [existingText stringByAppendingFormat:@"\n%@",
    incomingDataAsString];

  [self.textViewIncomingData setText:finalText];

  [incomingDataAsString release];

}
```

13. In the `buttonSendDataTapped:` action method, which gets called when the Send Data button is pressed, send some data (as `NSData`) to all players in the game (in this case, aside from the local player, only one other player) using the `sendData ToAllPlayers:withDataMode:error:` instance method of your match object, the `acceptedMatch` property of your root view controller:

```
- (IBAction)buttonSendDataTapped:(id)sender {

  NSString *dataToSend =
    [NSString stringWithFormat:@"Date = %@",
```

```
    [NSDate date]];

  NSData *data =
    [dataToSend dataUsingEncoding:NSUTF8StringEncoding];

  [self.acceptedMatch
    sendDataToAllPlayers:data
    withDataMode:GKMatchSendDataReliable
    error:nil];

}
```

14. Last but not least, in the viewDidUnload method of your view controller, make sure to set your outlet properties to nil in order to make sure the view's lifetime is properly handled in case of memory warnings getting sent by the iOS:

```
- (void)viewDidUnload{
  self.buttonSendData = nil;
  self.textViewIncomingData = nil;
  [super viewDidUnload];
}
```

We are all done. Let's run the app on two iOS devices and see what happens. What I'm going to demonstrate here is running the app on an iPad 2 and an iPhone 4. The iPad 2 version of the app will send an invite to the local player on the iPhone 4 while the app is not even open on the iPhone. Figure 1-18 shows what the iPhone player will see on her device.

Figure 1-18. An invitation from Game Center to initiate multiplayer game

number of two players and then one of the players gets disconnected, the expected PlayerCount method will return the value of 1, telling us that the match object expects one more player before it can start again. In the following code, assuming we are in a two-player match during which one player gets disconnected, we will stop the match all together:

```
/* The player state changed
 (eg. connected or disconnected) */
- (void)  match:(GKMatch *)match
        player:(NSString *)playerID
 didChangeState:(GKPlayerConnectionState)state{

  switch (state){

    case GKPlayerStateDisconnected:{

      if ([match expectedPlayerCount] > 0){
        [match disconnect];
      }
      break;

    }
  }

}
```

See Also

Recipe 1.17

Get even more for your money.

Join the O'Reilly Community, and register the O'Reilly books you own. It's free, and you'll get:

- $4.99 ebook upgrade offer
- 40% upgrade offer on O'Reilly print books
- Membership discounts on books and events
- Free lifetime updates to ebooks and videos
- Multiple ebook formats, DRM FREE
- Participation in the O'Reilly community
- Newsletters
- Account management
- 100% Satisfaction Guarantee

Signing up is easy:

1. **Go to: oreilly.com/go/register**
2. **Create an O'Reilly login.**
3. **Provide your address.**
4. **Register your books.**

Note: English-language books only

To order books online:
oreilly.com/store

For questions about products or an order:
orders@oreilly.com

To sign up to get topic-specific email announcements and/or news about upcoming books, conferences, special offers, and new technologies:
elists@oreilly.com

For technical questions about book content:
booktech@oreilly.com

To submit new book proposals to our editors:
proposals@oreilly.com

O'Reilly books are available in multiple DRM-free ebook formats. For more information:
oreilly.com/ebooks

O'REILLY®

Spreading the knowledge of innovators   oreilly.com